SMOOTH TRANSITIONS 4 TEENS

Career Education and Life-Skills Planning

DAVID AND MYRA VANDY

BALBOA.PRESS
A DIVISION OF HAY HOUSE

Balboa Press books may be ordered through booksellers or by contacting:

Balboa Press
A Division of Hay House
1663 Liberty Drive
Bloomington, IN 47403
www.balboapress.com
1 (877) 407-4847

Because of the dynamic nature of the Internet, any web addresses or links contained in this book may have changed since publication and may no longer be valid. The views expressed in this work are solely those of the author and do not necessarily reflect the views of the publisher, and the publisher hereby disclaims any responsibility for them.

The author of this book does not dispense medical advice or prescribe the use of any technique as a form of treatment for physical, emotional, or medical problems without the advice of a physician, either directly or indirectly. The intent of the author is only to offer information of a general nature to help you in your quest for emotional and spiritual well-being. In the event you use any of the information in this book for yourself, which is your constitutional right, the author and the publisher assume no responsibility for your actions.

Any people depicted in stock imagery provided by Getty Images are models, and such images are being used for illustrative purposes only. Certain stock imagery © Getty Images.

ISBN: 978-1-9822-1382-4 (sc)
ISBN: 978-1-9822-1381-7 (e)

Library of Congress Control Number: 2018912007

Print information available on the last page.

Balboa Press rev. date: 10/19/2018

Name:

_____

Address:

_____

_____

Phone: Email:

_____   _____

Other information:

_____

_____

_____

SMOOTH TRANSITIONS 4 TEENS Career/Education and Life Skills Planning

SMOOTH TRANSITIONS
4 TEENS
WILL HELP YOU:

1. Build Confidence in yourself

2. Decrease fear and worry about the future by taking one step at a time

3. Learn the steps and acquire the skills to prepare for life on your own

4. Set goals for yourself

5. Make realistic plans to help you reach your goals

6. Experiment with several career options before making a commitment

7. Develop financial security by saving and managing your money wisely

8. Build your resume'

9. Become the decision maker in your life

10. Create Your Perfect Life; Intend to succeed

SMOOTH TRANSITIONS
4
TEENS

*Is your Career and Job Interview
Portfolio*

Display Your Accomplishments!

"Everyone has inside of them

A piece of good news.

The good news is that you don't

know how GREAT you can be!

How much you can LOVE!

What you can ACCOMPLISH!

and

What your POTENTIAL is!"

Anne Frank

CONTENTS

INTRODUCTION

Do you want to know something? You have everything you need inside of you right now to create a happy, prosperous, and purposeful life. You have the ability to maintain a lifestyle and career that you enjoy and look forward to every day, that you can get excited about. If you are willing to take the steps, doing what your heart leads you to do you can inspire yourself, build your self-confidence and make a positive difference in this world. In short, **you can Create Your Perfect Life.**

Sometimes the hardest part of a project is getting started. Creating and planning for the future can seem like a giant-sized task. Many people ask, "Where do I start? I don't know what I want to do, or, what are the steps to get me there." Others may say "I know what I want to do, but don't know how to do the steps". **SMOOTH TRANSITIONS 4 TEENS will help you identify the steps.**

Take a few minutes to page through SMOOTH TRANSITIONS 4 TEENS to familiarize yourself with its contents. You will find the **Introductory Survey**, which will help you think about things that are important to you, so you can form a rough idea about what you might like to try for a possible career. This is followed by a visioning exercise called **10 Steps to Creating Your Perfect Life**. This exercise will show you how to create what you would like to see happen in your future.

The next part of SMOOTH TRANSITIONS 4 TEENS consists of **15** categories, where plenty of space is provided to record your thoughts, ideas and experiences that correspond with each category. From education and employment to home management, leisure/recreation, legal issues, and much more you will begin to take the steps along the path to your unique future.

Next are 24 **Monthly Planning** pages. Here you can record the things you will accomplish during the upcoming months. It is recommended that you make monthly plans to better organize yourself. **The most important thing is to get started.**

By investing some time to really think through the questions in the Introductory Survey and by regularly repeating the 10 Steps exercise, **your future will become clearer to you.** So often we allow time to pass with no real thought of planning for the future. Life events happen, circumstances change and a life which we may not particularly want or prefer has somehow been formed around us or for us. This need not be the case for you. As you invest time, creative thought and planning for your future, **SMOOTH TRANSITIONS 4 TEENS will help you develop the life you really want to have. You deserve the best!**

When your goals and ideas for the future change, SMOOTH TRANSITIONS 4 TEENS can help you accommodate those changes. As you continue to make decisions for your future, you will most likely go through a period of trial and error. A career or education path which might have looked good six months or a year ago may be replaced by new choices as you learn and experience new things. You may find something else you really enjoy. For this reason, there is a second survey following the first one. When you need to modify plans, complete the second survey when it is appropriate for you. This will help you reassess and refocus your efforts for your new career or education path. **Exploring career possibilities** is important for everyone. When you explore potential career possibilities by **volunteering** or by serving as an **intern** or through **paid work**, you will have more information and greater life experience to **develop clearer goals for yourself**.

Calendars are located at the back of SMOOTH TRANSITIONS 4 TEENS to help you organize and plan wisely. Using the calendars will help you plan ahead logically and practically allowing you to enter other things you will want to fit into your schedule. The task ahead of you will be very rewarding and at times challenging. You will accomplish much as you begin to create a plan for yourself, **working it step by step**.

A lot of your time will be spent learning and gathering information by computer or phone, which provide instant information. You can learn almost anything online. The benefits of electronic devices are fantastic. The benefits of your hard copy of SMOOTH TRANSITIONS 4 TEENS are very real and can greatly complement digital information. **SMOOTH TRANSITIONS 4 TEENS can serve as your portfolio when you interview with potential employers, where everything you have accomplished can be easily shown and described.** Whether you are developing ideas alone or with a helper, you can sit down and look at the big picture more easily by having SMOOTH TRANSITIONS 4 TEENS right in front of you, where everything is immediately at your fingertips. In short, it will help you stay organized and to see, touch, and show what you have accomplished. It will help keep you motivated!

With assistance and guidance from the many people in your life who are in positions to help you, you will accomplish your goals by working methodically to achieve them. As you explore career and education options, putting forth the effort to acquire necessary skills, you will **empower yourself,** gain confidence and increasingly **become the decision maker, creating the life _you_ want to have. The Sky is the Limit!**

"All you need is the plan, the road map and the courage to press on to Your Destination"

Earl Nightingale

HOW TO USE SMOOTH TRANSITIONS 4 TEENS

Not all objectives in SMOOTH TRANSITIONS 4 TEENS need to be completed by everyone using the planner. Complete the objectives that are most important to you first. **Skip those which do not apply to you. Your own personal objectives**, which may be recorded in the Personal Objectives category are those that **are most important and unique to you**. These ideas can be a cornerstone around which the other objectives are built. If you don't have any personal objectives, especially when you first begin to use SMOOTH TRANSITIONS 4 TEENS, that's okay. You can develop them later.

- **Browse through SMOOTH TRANSITIONS 4 TEENS** and become familiar with it.
- Complete the **Introductory Survey** with a helper, if possible.
- Do the **10 Steps to Creating Your Perfect Life** exercise. Get into the habit of repeating your vision aloud and in your mind over and over, as if it already exists and you are living it **now**.
- Use YouTube and other online learning tools often to educate yourself about almost anything that can help you with completing objectives. This is especially helpful if you are working mostly on your own.
- **Take your time** - do what you feel comfortable with as you go. **Keep your momentum going; keep trying! If you find that you have lost momentum, start again. Make this promise to yourself and keep it. You will be so glad you did!**
- **Do not let the fact that you may be older or younger than a teenager stop you from using SMOOTH TRANSITIONS 4 TEENS. This book will benefit a wide age range of users.**

At the back of the book you will find calendars.

Number the calendars as shown below, starting with the month you begin using SMOOTH TRANSITIONS 4 TEENS. For example, if you start SMOOTH TRANSITIONS 4 TEENS in January, mark January as Month 1 as in the example below. If you start SMOOTH TRANSITIONS 4 TEENS in February, mark February as Month 1, etc. This will help build a time frame for completing your monthly plans.

1 — JANUARY 2025

S	M	T	W	TH	F	S
			1	2	3	4
5	6	7	8	9	10	11
12	13	14	15	16	17	18
19	20	21	22	23	24	25
26	27	28	29	30	31	

2 — FEBRUARY 2025

S	M	T	W	TH	F	S
						1
2	3	4	5	6	7	8
9	10	11	12	13	14	15
16	17	18	19	20	21	22
23	24	25	26	27	28	

3 — MARCH 2025

S	M	T	W	TH	F	S
						1
2	3	4	5	6	7	8
9	10	11	12	13	14	15
16	17	18	19	20	21	22
23	24	25	26	27	28	29
30	31					

4 — APRIL 2025

S	M	T	W	TH	F	S
		1	2	3	4	5
6	7	8	9	10	11	12
13	14	15	16	17	18	19
20	21	22	23	24	25	26
27	28	29	30			

5 — MAY 2025

S	M	T	W	TH	F	S
				1	2	3
4	5	6	7	8	9	10
11	12	13	14	15	16	17
18	19	20	21	22	23	24
25	26	27	28	29	30	31

6 — JUNE 2025

S	M	T	W	TH	F	S
1	2	3	4	5	6	7
8	9	10	11	12	13	14
15	16	17	18	19	20	21
22	23	24	25	26	27	28
29	30					

7 — JULY 2025

S	M	T	W	TH	F	S
		1	2	3	4	5
6	7	8	9	10	11	12
13	14	15	16	17	18	19
20	21	22	23	24	25	26
27	28	29	30	31		

8 — AUGUST 2025

S	M	T	W	TH	F	S
					1	2
3	4	5	6	7	8	9
10	11	12	13	14	15	16
17	18	19	20	21	22	23
24	25	26	27	28	29	30

9 — SEPTEMBER 2025

S	M	T	W	TH	F	S
	1	2	3	4	5	6
7	8	9	10	11	12	13
14	15	16	17	18	19	20
21	22	23	24	25	26	27
28	29	30				

10 — OCTOBER 2025

S	M	T	W	TH	F	S
			1	2	3	4
5	6	7	8	9	10	11
12	13	14	15	16	17	18
19	20	21	22	23	24	25
26	27	28	29	30	31	

11 — NOVEMBER 2025

S	M	T	W	TH	F	S
						1
2	3	4	5	6	7	8
9	10	11	12	13	14	15
16	17	18	19	20	21	22
23	24	25	26	27	28	29
30						

12 — DECEMBER 2025

S	M	T	W	TH	F	S
	1	2	3	4	5	6
7	8	9	10	11	12	13
14	15	16	17	18	19	20
21	22	23	24	25	26	27
28	29	30	31			

Enter the appropriate month and year at the top of each of the 24 **Monthly Plans** pages as shown below, starting with the month you begin using SMOOTH TRANSITIONS 4 TEENS.

MONTHLY PLANS

Month # 1   Month: <u>January</u>   Year: <u>2025</u>

<u>WEEK # 1:</u>

<u>WEEK # 2:</u>

<u>WEEK # 3:</u>

<u>WEEK # 4:</u>

<u>WEEK # 5:</u>

MONTHLY PLANS

Month # 2   Month: <u>February</u>   Year: <u>2025</u>

<u>WEEK # 1:</u>

<u>WEEK # 2:</u>

<u>WEEK # 3:</u>

<u>WEEK # 4:</u>

<u>WEEK # 5:</u>

By completing the above steps, you have done something very important for yourself. <u>The task of preparing for your future has been distilled down to a handful of workable steps.</u> You have thought through what is important to you, creating a beginning vision for your future. You have established a rough time frame to complete specific tasks. <u>These are the steps along your path for a smooth transition to adulthood</u>. Be patient with yourself, keep trying, stay positive and enjoy the journey.

*"The
starting point
in
every
transformation
is to
think
differently"*

John McKnight and Peter Block

Introductory Survey

Have a helper ask the questions, if possible, and record your answers. Date:

1. Which school subjects do (or did) you like best?

2. What are your hobbies and interests? What do you do in your free time?

3. Have you done any volunteer work? If yes, where and when?

4. Have you ever had a job? Where did you work and how long did you work there?

    Best thing(s) about your work:

5. What problems in your town or the world need to be fixed and how would you solve these problems?

6. What is happening in the world or your town that you think is good, that you want to support? What could you do to give your support to these things or situations?

7. What are you naturally good at?

8. Do you work better by yourself, with another person, with small groups of people or in large groups?

9. Would you like to own your own business, work for a large corporation or for a small company?

10. Would you like to live near where you live now, somewhere else, in another part of the country, or in another country?

11. List the two people you admire most. They may be people you know personally, someone famous or someone from history.

What can you do to accomplish similar things, or to accomplish a goal you may have?

When you have completed the survey, ask your helper to tell a descriptive, positive story about you, using the information you provided. If you completed it alone tell the story aloud to yourself or to another, if you like.

2ND SURVEY

Have a helper ask the questions, if possible, and record your answers. Date:

1. Which school subjects do (or did) you like best?

2. What are your hobbies and interests? What do you do in your free time?

3. Have you done any volunteer work? If yes, where and when?

4. Have you ever had a job? Where did you work and how long did you work there?

    Best thing(s) about your work:

5. What problems in your town or the world need to be fixed and how would you solve these problems?

6. What is happening in the world or your town that you think is good, that you want to support? What could you do to give your support to these things or situations?

7. What are you naturally good at?

8. Do you work better by yourself, with another person, with small groups of people or in large groups?

9. Would you like to own your own business, work for a large corporation or for a small company?

10. Would you like to live near where you live now, somewhere else, in another region of the country or in another country?

11. List the two people you admire most. They may be people you know personally, someone famous or someone from history.

What can you do to accomplish similar things, or to accomplish a goal you may have?

When you have completed the survey, ask your helper to tell a descriptive, positive story about you, or speak it aloud to yourself or to another using the information you provided. Compare how your answers might have changed from the first time you took the survey.

*"The Universe is a big
Dream Machine,
turning out dreams
and transforming them
into reality,
and
our own dreams
are inextricably woven
into the overall scheme of things."*

Deepak Chopra

10 Steps To Creating Your Perfect Life

1. Make a list of what you want to do with your future, what you want to have, what you want to be, and the kind of person you want to be.

    * Brainstorm; let your imagination run free, and let your heart and feelings guide you. *

2. Create a picture in your mind. Picture yourself working in the career you are meant for. * Relax, observe yourself as if you are watching yourself in a movie. *

10 Steps To Creating Your Perfect Life

3. See yourself doing this work now. It's perfect for you!

   * How are you dressed, where are you living, how are you feeling?

4. Think of it in the present. *It already exists. *

5. Picture yourself calm and relaxed, accomplishing much without strain or excessive effort.

   * Become the observer of these scenes! *

6. Picture yourself taking practical steps to accomplish your goals; intend to achieve them. <u>Make this promise to yourself!</u>

   * List some steps and picture yourself doing them. Think deeply about this! *

10 STEPS TO CREATING YOUR PERFECT LIFE

7. See yourself achieving your goals and receiving the rewards you have earned. * How much do you earn?

    * What are you driving?
    * What does your house look like?
    * Are you making investments?
    * Who do you spend time with?

    Congratulate yourself NOW!

8. Create a vision board for yourself.

    * Cut out pictures, and phrases from magazines or other places which show your vision and attach them to your vision board.
    * Place it where you will see it every day.
    * Make positive statements about your vision aloud as you look at it.
    **Observe how you feel about yourself, now that you have accomplished your goals **

9. Write out your vision in a sentence or two.

    * Add it to your vision board*

10. Speak and mentally rehearse your vision * EVERY DAY*, focusing on it in a relaxed way*

    * Modify your vision as is appropriate for you*

VISION
DO SOMETHING EACH DAY
TO MATERIALIZE IT

"Believe you can

and

you're halfway

there"

President Theodore Roosevelt

PLANNING
CATEGORIES

EDUCATION

Objective # 1:

Earn your high school diploma or GED.

Record Information:

Objective # 2:

Obtain your high school transcripts.

Record Information:

Objective # 3:

Seek out alternate ways to earn high school or higher education credits.
Talk to teachers, counselors, principals; do YouTube and other online research

Record Information:

Objective # 4:

Participate in educational field trips.

* This could be a school organized trip to a business or community facility or a trip with family or friends. Vacations are often very educational and can spark your interest in a potential career or education path or even a place you may choose to live in the future*

Record locations, dates, experiences:

Objective #5:

Interview professionals in areas of your educational interest.

Initiate conversations and tell them what your interests are, ask about what they studied, where they went to school and the steps they took along the way to get where they are now. You will most likely find that people will be happy to share their journey with you

Record experiences, names, dates, etc.:

Objective # 6:

Do internet higher education research (apprenticeships, vocational schools, community colleges, or universities).

Talk to guidance counselors at your present school and at other schools you would like to attend

Record information:

Objective # 7:

Apply to schools and research available financial aid resources: scholarships, work study, FAFSA (Free Application for Federal Student Aid), grants, student loans, etc.

Do financial aid research 18 months before you will need it, or as soon as possible. Get help filling out forms, if you can, and watch online videos for help

Record information:

Objective # 8:

Visit schools of your choice (colleges, universities, community colleges, trade schools).

Thoroughly check out and read reviews for any school you are considering. Speak with a student advisor, (make an appointment ahead of time), take a tour of the facility, which are often led by current students. Talk to as many other students as you can; see what kind of feeling you get

Record information:

Objective # 9

List schools attended, with dates attended, addresses and contact information. *Take SMOOTH TRANSITIONS 4 TEENS with you when you fill out job applications or go on an interview. You will need your education history to complete job applications*

Name and Address of school:_____

_____

Telephone Number:_____

Website:_____

Contact Person(s):_____

Dates attended: FROM: _____ TO:_____

Last Grade:_____

Date of Graduation:_____

Degree or Certification Earned:_____

Awards or Recognitions:_____

_____

- -

Name and Address of school:_____

_____

Telephone Number:_____

Website:_____

Contact Person(s):_____

Dates attended: FROM: _____ TO:_____

Last Grade:_____

Date of Graduation:_____

Degree or Certification Earned:_____

Awards or Recognitions:_____

_____

Objective # 9:

List schools attended, with dates attended, addresses and contact information.

Name and Address of school:_____

_____

Telephone Number:_____

Website:_____

Contact Person(s):_____

Dates attended: FROM: _____ TO:_____

Last Grade:_____

Date of Graduation:_____

Degree or Certification Earned:_____

Awards or Recognitions:_____

_____

- -

Name and Address of school:_____

_____

Telephone Number:_____

Website:_____

Contact Person(s):_____

Dates attended: FROM: _____ TO:_____

Last Grade:_____

Date of Graduation:_____

Degree or Certification Earned:_____

Awards or Recognitions:_____

_____

Objective # 9:

List schools attended, with dates attended, addresses and contact information.

Name and Address of school: _____

_____

Telephone Number: _____

Website: _____

Contact Person(s): _____

Dates attended: FROM: _____ **TO:** _____

Last Grade: _____

Date of Graduation: _____

Degree or Certification Earned: _____

Awards or Recognitions: _____

_____

- -

Name and Address of school: _____

_____

Telephone Number: _____

Website: _____

Contact Person(s): _____

Dates attended: FROM: _____ **TO:** _____

Last Grade: _____

Date of Graduation: _____

Degree or Certification Earned: _____

Awards or Recognitions: _____

_____

Objective # 9

List schools attended, with dates attended, addresses and contact information.

Name and Address of school:_____

_____

Telephone Number:_____

Website:_____

Contact Person(s):_____

Dates attended: FROM: _____ TO:_____

Last Grade:_____

Date of Graduation:_____

Degree or Certification Earned:_____

Awards or Recognitions:_____

_____

- -

Name and Address of school:_____

_____

Telephone Number:_____

Website:_____

Contact Person(s):_____

Dates attended: FROM: _____ TO:_____

Last Grade:_____

Date of Graduation:_____

Degree or Certification Earned:_____

Awards or Recognitions:_____

_____

Objective # 10:

Four Year Personal Program of Study

Enter goals and information below for your <u>FIRST</u> of four years Personal Program of Study. This may be for high school, college or vocational-technical school.

YEAR 1:_____

<u>**GOAL 1:**</u>   Date Completed: _____

<u>**GOAL 2:**</u>   Date Completed: _____

<u>**GOAL 3:**</u>   Date Completed: _____

Objective # 10:

Four Year Personal Program of Study

Enter information below for your <u>FIRST</u> of four years Personal Program of Study. This may be for high school, college or vocational-technical school. * Include grades and GPA, Grade Point Average

	Date Begin	Date End	Course Name Course Number	Teacher Name	# of Units/ Credits	Required/ Elective Enter R or E	Grade Earned
1st Semester							
							GPA
2nd Semester							
							GPA
1st Summer Session							
							GPA
2nd Summer Session							GPA

Objective # 10:

Four Year Personal Program of Study

Enter goals and information below for your <u>SECOND</u> of four years Personal Program of Study. This may be for high school, college or vocational-technical school.

YEAR 2: _____

<u>GOAL 1:</u>   Date Completed: _____

<u>GOAL 2:</u>   Date Completed: _____

<u>GOAL 3:</u>   Date Completed: _____

Objective # 10:

Four Year Personal Program of Study

Enter information below for your <u>SECOND</u> of four years Personal Program of Study. This may be for high school, college or vocational-technical school. * Include grades and GPA, Grade Point Average*

	Date Begin	Date End	Course Name Course Number	Teacher Name	# of Units/ Credits	Required/ Elective Enter R or E	Grade Earned
1st Semester							
							GPA
2nd Semester							
							GPA
1st Summer Session							
							GPA
2nd Summer Session							
							GPA

Objective # 10:

Four Year Personal Program of Study

Enter goals and information below for your <u>THIRD</u> of four years Personal Program of Study. This may be for high school, college or vocational-technical school.

YEAR 3: _____

<u>**GOAL 1:**</u>   Date Completed: _____

<u>**GOAL 2:**</u>   Date Completed: _____

<u>**GOAL 3:**</u>   Date Completed: _____

Objective # 10:

Four Year Personal Program of Study

Enter information below for your <u>THIRD</u> of four years Personal Program of Study. This may be for high school, college or vocational-technical school. * Include grades and GPA, Grade Point Average*

	Date Begin	Date End	Course Name Course Number	Teacher Name	# of Units/ Credits	Required/ Elective Enter R or E	Grade Earned
1st Semester							
							GPA
2nd Semester							
							GPA
1st Summer Session							
							GPA
2nd Summer Session							
							GPA

Objective # 10:

Four Year Personal Program of Study

Enter goals and information below for your <u>FOURTH</u> of four years Personal Program of Study. This may be for high school, college or vocational-technical school.

YEAR 4: _____

<u>GOAL 1:</u>   **Date Completed:** _____

<u>GOAL 2:</u>   **Date Completed:** _____

<u>GOAL 3:</u>   **Date Completed:** _____

Objective # 10:

Four Year Personal Program of Study

Enter information below for your <u>FOURTH</u> of four years Personal Program of Study. This may be for high school, college or vocational-technical school. *Include grades and GPA; Grade Point Average*

	Date Begin	Date End	Course Name Course Number	Teacher Name	# of Units/ Credits	Required/ Elective Enter R or E	Grade Earned
1st Semester							
							GPA
2nd Semester							
							GPA
1st Summer Session							GPA
2nd Summer Session							GPA

Objective # 11:

BEYOND YOUR FOUR-YEAR PERSONAL PROGRAM OF STUDY

Enter information below for a <u>FIFTH</u> year of high school, or college, graduate school or vocational-technical education.

School Name:_____ Year 5: _____

	Date Begin	Date End	Course Name Course Number	Teacher Name	# of Units/ Credits	Required/ Elective Enter R or E	Grade Earned
1st Semester							
							GPA
2nd Semester							
							GPA
1st Summer Session							
							GPA
2nd Summer Session							
							GPA

Objective # 11:

BEYOND YOUR FOUR-YEAR PERSONAL PROGRAM OF STUDY

Enter information below for a <u>FIFTH</u> year of high school, or college, graduate school or vocational-technical education.

YEAR 5: _____

<u>GOAL 1:</u>   Date:_____ Date Completed:_____

<u>GOAL 2:</u>   Date:_____ Date Completed:_____

<u>GOAL 3:</u>   Date:_____ Date Completed:_____

"Two roads diverged in the wood

and I took the one less traveled

and that has made

all the difference"

Robert Frost

Additional Notes and Information

Longmont Mural—courtesy of City of Longmont, CO and Gamma Acosta (artist)

*"Keep your face always to the sunshine –
and the shadows will always be behind you"*

Walt Whitman

Additional Notes and Information

*"I know of no more encouraging fact
than the unquestionable ability of man
to elevate his life by a conscious endeavor."*

Henry David Thoreau

EMPLOYMENT

Objective # 1:

Collect necessary documents and record information before you look for a job.

Make sure to have your education history information which you recorded in <u>Education Objective #9 above. Take SMOOTH TRANSITIONS 4 TEENS with you when you fill out job applications or go on a job interview. You will need to enter your education history to fill out a job application. Show what you have accomplished; the interviewer will be impressed</u>

Social Security card

* Contact the local Social Security office in your town and they will tell you the steps for obtaining either a new or replacement social security card. <u>Always protect your social security number from identity theft</u>*

ID card

* Contact the local Department of Motor Vehicles (DMV or MVD) and they will tell you the steps for obtaining a state issued ID card*

Employment history with contact information

<u>Take SMOOTH TRANSITIONS 4 TEENS with you to job interviews, and when you go to fill out job applications.</u> You will be totally prepared by having your employment history recorded and right in front of you. This information is recorded in <u>Employment Objective #11 below.</u> You will set yourself apart during an interview with <u>SMOOTH TRANSITIONS 4 TEENS, your career planning portfolio</u> in hand, as you confidently show the interviewer all you have accomplished

Objective # 2:

Write your resume'; *Update it at least every year.

The internet or library will help you. Sometimes libraries have free classes in resume' writing*

Record dates resume' first completed and updated:

Objective # 3:

Search internet/ newspaper classified ads regularly.

* Record possibilities and check them out*

Dates:

Objective # 4:

Search the internet for employment ideas and possibilities.

Record important information only; create a file in your computer or phone

Objective # 5:

Obtain employment applications (from the person who does the hiring, if possible).

Record name, contact information, etc.

Objective # 6:

Request letters of recommendation from your employer before you move on to your next job.

<u>You will always need letters of recommendation when you apply for a job</u>. Make sure you give your employers at least two weeks' notice before you leave a job. Do your best to leave any job positively, even if you believe you were not treated well

Make copies and record names, dates, etc.

Objective # 7:

Practice job interviewing.

*Rehearse out loud with a friend, or in front of a mirror. Use the internet, (i.e. YouTube) to view examples of interviews, then practice some more. <u>You will do great</u> *

Notes, dates:

Objective # 8:

Participate in employment field trips. *Talk to potential employers by yourself, if possible.

Record names, dates, locations and contact information*

Objective # 9:

Go on job interviews.

Dress well; be prepared to tell why you believe you are the best candidate for the position you are interviewing for. Why are you the one they should hire? Tell about your goals, plans and accomplishments. <u>Smile, be confident and positive, and let the wonderful you that you are shine through</u>

Notes, dates, locations, contact information:

Objective # 10:

Practice job maintenance skills. <u>*Appearance, punctuality, accuracy, working as a team member; do these things consistently.</u> If you are going to be late, are sick or will miss work for any reason, give as much notice as possible to your employer. If you need time off from work, ask permission well ahead of time*

Make notes:

Objective # 11:

Work at least part-time. List your employment history below. Enter dates of employment.

Record information:

Start Date: _____   **End Date:**_____

Business Name:_____

_____

Business Address:_____

_____

Telephone number/website:_____

_____

Supervisor(s) name(s):_____

_____

Your job title:_____

Job Description:_____

_____

_____

Average number of hours worked per week:_____

Starting Salary: _____   **Ending Salary:** _____

Objective # 11:

Work at least part-time. List your employment history below. Enter dates of employment.

Record information:

Start Date: _____ End Date:_____

Business Name:_____

_____

Business Address:_____

_____

Telephone number/website:_____

_____

Supervisor(s) name(s):_____

_____

Your job title:_____

Job Description:_____

_____

_____

Average number of hours worked per week:_____

Starting Salary: _____ Ending Salary: _____

Objective # 11:

Work at least part-time. List your employment history below. Enter dates of employment.

Record information:

Start Date: _____   **End Date:** _____

Business Name: _____

_____

Business Address: _____

_____

Telephone number/website: _____

_____

Supervisor(s) name(s): _____

_____

Your job title: _____

Job Description: _____

_____

_____

Average number of hours worked per week: _____

Starting Salary: _____   **Ending Salary:** _____

Objective # 11:

Work at least part-time. List your employment history below. Enter dates of employment.

Record information:

Start Date: _____   **End Date:** _____

Business Name: _____

_____

Business Address: _____

_____

Telephone number/website: _____

_____

Supervisor(s) name(s): _____

_____

Your job title: _____

Job Description: _____

_____

_____

Average number of hours worked per week: _____

Starting Salary: _____   **Ending Salary:** _____

Objective # 12:

Explore apprenticeship programs online and by visiting, if possible.

Ask questions; do some research and prepare ahead of time

Record information:

Objective # 13:

Spend one day working with someone who works in your area of interest (job shadow).

Be patient, polite, and inquisitive. Learn as much as you can about where you will job shadow before you start

Record experiences:

Objective # 14:

Interview professionals in your areas of interest.

Talk to people you know for help. Take notes, prepare ahead of time, do online research

Record names, dates and experiences:

"Your work is going to fill a large part of your life, and the only way to be truly satisfied is to do what you believe is great work. And the only way to do great work is to love what you do. If you haven't found it yet, keep looking. Don't settle. As with all matters of the heart, you'll know when you find it."

Steve Jobs

"Knowing is not enough; we must apply."
Willing is not enough; we must do..."

Johann Wolfgang Van Goethe

Additional Notes and Information

Additional Notes and Information

FOOD AND NUTRITION

Objective # 1:

Plan out well-balanced meals.

Write it out below

5 Basic Food Groups

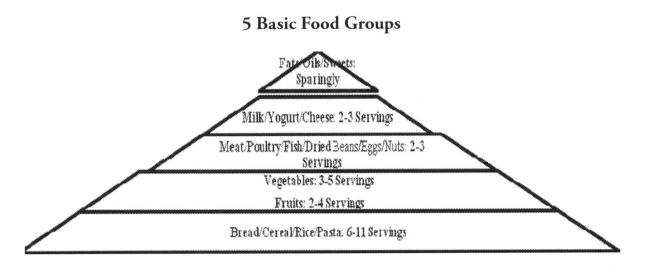

Meal One:

Objective # 1:

Plan out well-balanced meals. *Write them out below*

<u>Meal Two:</u>

<u>Meal Three:</u>

Objective # 2　　　　Write a grocery list for the week; practice.　　　Date:

FRESH FRUITS VEGETABLES	MEAT/POULTRY FISH/BEANS	DAIRY PRODUCTS

CANNED GOODS	SNACKS/BEVERAGES	FROZEN FOOD

PAPER PRODUCTS/ CLEANING SUPPLIES	HYGIENE PRODUCTS	OTHER

Objective # 2   Write a grocery list for the week; practice.   Date:

FRESH FRUITS VEGETABLES	MEAT/POULTRY FISH/BEANS	DAIRY PRODUCTS

CANNED GOODS	SNACKS/BEVERAGES	FROZEN FOOD

PAPER PRODUCTS/ CLEANING SUPPLIES	HYGIENE PRODUCTS	OTHER

Objective # 2   Write a grocery list for the week; practice.   Date:

FRESH FRUITS VEGETABLES	MEAT/POULTRY FISH/BEANS	DAIRY PRODUCTS

CANNED GOODS	SNACKS/BEVERAGES	FROZEN FOOD

PAPER PRODUCTS/ CLEANING SUPPLIES	HYGIENE PRODUCTS	OTHER

Objective # 3:

Shop for food wisely: quality, value.

Check store advertisements for sales and coupons, read labels. Check your receipts for accuracy. Take your grocery list with you. Go with an experienced shopper to start with, if possible

Dates, notes:

Objective # 4:

Learn to cook well and safely for yourself; practice. *Talk to people you know and ask them for help. Watch YouTube and other online videos*

Record dates and describe what you cooked:

Objective # 5:

Prepare and preserve meals ahead of time. *Freeze in plastic containers for quick, easy meals when you don't have time to prepare food. You will eat better and save money. Experiment with foods you normally like to eat*

Notes:

Objective # 6:

Invite a friend over for a dinner which you have prepared once every two months, or more often if you like.

* Describe the meal*

Record names and dates:

"For all our insight, obstinate habits do not disappear until replaced by other habits...
No amount of confession, and no amount of explaining can make a crooked plant grow straight;
it must be trained upon the trellis by the gardener's art..."

Carl Jung

Additional Notes and Information

*"Start by doing what's necessary,
then do what's possible;
and suddenly
you are doing the impossible".*

Francis of Assisi

FUTURE
COMMUNITY
CONNECTIONS

Objective # 1:

Go online and search newspapers for employment, housing and volunteer possibilities for the location(s) you may live when you are on your own.

Website:_____

Website: _____

Website: _____

Website: _____

Newspaper name:_____ Date:_____

<u>Employment Possibilities:</u>

<u>Housing Possibilities:</u>

<u>Volunteer Possibilities</u>

Objective # 2:

Research a team, group or organization you would like to join in the location you will live when you are on your own.

Expand your network of support; intentionally connect with others who are outside of groups you currently associate with. <u>If you step out of your comfort zone, you may discover things about yourself that you may never have realized before and you'll probably meet some great people</u>

Dates, notes:

Objective # 3:

Visit a potential volunteer site of your choice in the location you will live when you are on your own.

Arrange to contribute 3 hours or more per month when you live there. <u>You may be surprised at the unexpected benefits, recognition and support you might receive</u>

Record information:

Objective # 4:

Become familiar with your future home.

*Visit places that will be important to you. * Check out schools, churches, parks, hiking/ biking trails, rec centers, stores, restaurants, your voting location, the bank you will use, places where you may have your car serviced, the location of your doctor and medical facilities, etc.*

Collect information:

Objective # 5   **Date(s):**_____

Obtain a map of your future hometown and familiarize yourself with main roads and landmarks. Highlight important routes and places.

* Learn how to read a map, watch videos, ask for help from someone who knows how to read a map; sometimes electronics fail. <u>If you will be traveling to a location where you think you may lose cell phone reception you can bring directions up on your phone and write them down in the event you need them</u>*

*"If you always put limits on everything you
do - physical or anything else,
it will spread into your work and into your life.*

There are no limits.

*There are only plateaus, and you must not stay there.
You must go beyond them".*

Bruce Lee

*"The moment one definitely commits oneself,
then Providence moves too.
All sorts of things occur to help one that would
never otherwise have occurred…
Unforeseen incidents, meetings, and material assistance, which
no man could have dreamed would have come his way.*

Johann Wolfgang von Goethe

HEALTH

Objective # 1

Practice daily personal hygiene, including dental care, showering and hair care. * Maintain positive mental hygiene by deciding to keep a positive attitude*

Objective # 2

Make a habit of keeping your clothes clean, laundering them weekly, at a minimum.

Objective # 3

Feed yourself a healthy diet. * Food is your best medicine*

Objective # 4

Educate yourself about sexually transmitted disease and pregnancy prevention. * Talk to people you trust in addition to peers and do online research. Educate yourself about planning when and if you want to become somebody's parent. Are you ready and able to support a child? Smart choices now will preserve your options for your future*

Think ahead!

NOTES:

Objective #5:

Create or buy a first aid kit for your home. *Keep it available*

Items, dates:

Objective # 6:

Understand how to utilize health care benefits and investigate services at a clinic in the location you will live after you are on your own.

Know what costs you will be responsible for

Record information:

Objective # 7:

Visit community hospital and clinic locations you will use.

Record names, addresses and phone numbers:

Objective # 8:

Investigate and know how to utilize your local emergency services. * <u>Save emergency numbers in your phone</u>. Know the route to the emergency room so in case it is ever needed, you will know how to get there before an emergency*

Record information:

Objective # 9:

Check out counseling services, if you think you can benefit from counseling. *Do online research and check reviews*

Record information:

Objective # 10:

Join a support group specific to an area in which you may want support or need assistance.

* Research options online*

Record information:

*"Happiness is not something you
postpone for the future;
it is something you design
for the present"*

Jim Rohn

*"The battles that count aren't the ones for gold medals.
The struggles within yourself-
the invisible battles inside all of us-
that's where it's at."*

Jesse Owens

"What is necessary to change a person is to change his awareness of himself"

Abraham Maslow

HOME MANAGEMENT

Objective # 1:   Date(s):_____

Learn about your community housing resources online, in newspapers, on school bulletin boards or from someone you know.

Record Information:

Objective# 2:

Decide where you want to live. * List the positives and negatives*

<u>Positives</u>   <u>Negatives</u>

Objective # 3:

Research housing/rental websites and newspaper classified ads.

Check out several neighborhoods. Talk to friends and relatives; make sure you know what you can afford

See Home Management Objective # 7 below, Figuring your housing costs

Objective # 4:

Look for a place to live well before you will need it.

Know what is included in rental agreements you may sign. Talk to potential future neighbors if they are out and about and ask them what the neighborhood is like. Shop around and compare

Notes:

Objective # 5:

Ask questions; know your landlord's and your responsibilities - *Ask for a copy of the lease. Read it and consult with someone you trust, before you sign anything. <u>Take your time, shop around</u>*

Objective # 6:

Practice basic home repairs where you are living now. *Ask someone to help you and help someone else out who could use <u>your</u> help. <u>This is a great way to build relationships and learn</u>. Buy a basic small tool kit so you can take care of every day repairs.

Learn how to use a fire extinguisher; watch videos*

Record tasks, dates:

Objective # 7:   Date(s):_____

Figure your housing costs (including utilities, deposits, renter's insurance, furnishings) <u>before</u> you sign a lease. *You may be required to pay first and last months' rent up front or a substantial deposit. <u>Utilities usually require a deposit before starting service unless utilities are included in your rent</u>*

TOTAL PERSONAL HOUSING COSTS

<u>First Month</u>	<u>Every Month</u>
RENT:	RENT:
Electric:	Electric:
Water:	Water:
Gas:	Gas:
Phone:	Phone:
Cable:	Cable:
SECURITY DEPOSIT:	
OTHER DEPOSITS: (phone, electric, gas, water)	
RENTER'S INSURANCE: (optional)	RENTER'S INSURANCE (optional)
FURNITURE:	
KITCHEN SUPPLIES:	
OTHER EXPENSES:	OTHER EXPENSES:
TOTAL:_____	TOTAL: _____

Objective # 7:

Figure your housing costs (including utilities, deposits, renter's insurance, furnishings) <u>before</u> you sign a lease. *You may be required to pay first and last months' rent up front or a substantial deposit. <u>Utilities usually require a deposit before starting service unless utilities are included in your rent</u>*

TOTAL PERSONAL HOUSING COSTS

<u>First Month</u>	<u>Every Month</u>
RENT:	RENT:
Electric:	Electric:
Water:	Water:
Gas:	Gas:
Phone:	Phone:
Cable:	Cable:
SECURITY DEPOSIT:	
OTHER DEPOSITS: (phone, electric, gas, water)	
RENTER'S INSURANCE: (optional)	RENTER'S INSURANCE (optional)
FURNITURE:	
KITCHEN SUPPLIES:	
OTHER EXPENSES:	OTHER EXPENSES:
TOTAL:_____	TOTAL: _____

Objective # 8   Date(s):_____

Think through and write out how you will maintain your home **without** roommates.
Include responsibilities, costs, etc.

HOW I WILL MAINTAIN MY HOME WITHOUT ROOMMATES

My Responsibilities:

Objective # 8   Date(s):_____

Think through and write out how you will maintain your home <u>without</u> roommates (responsibilities, costs, etc.)

HOW I WILL MAINTAIN MY HOME <u>WITHOUT</u> ROOMMATES

<u>My Costs:</u>

Beginning   **Monthly**   **Other**

_____   _____   _____

TOTALS

Objective # 8   Date(s):_____

Think through and write out how you will maintain your home <u>with</u> roommates including division of responsibilities, costs, etc.

HOW I WILL MAINTAIN MY HOME <u>WITH</u> ROOMMATES

<u>**My Responsibilities:**</u>   <u>**My Roommate's Responsibilities**</u>

Objective # 8   Date(s):_____

Think through and write out how you will maintain your home <u>with</u> roommates including division of responsibilities, costs, etc.

HOW I WILL MAINTAIN MY HOME <u>WITH</u> ROOMMATES

<u>My Costs:</u>   <u>My Roommate's Costs:</u>

Beginning   Monthly   Other   Beginning   Monthly   Other

_____ _____ _____ _____ _____ _____

TOTALS

Objective # 9

Choose your roommates wisely: *Write out and agree upon house rules and responsibilities including costs - before moving in with anyone. Every roommate signs the agreement*

HOUSE RULES AND RESPONSIBILITIES: I (we) agree to abide by the following house rules:

CHORES AND RESPONSIBILITIES	NAME:	NAME:
Kitchen:		
Floors:		
Trash:		
Laundry:		
Other:		
EXPENSES:		
Rent:		
Utilities:		
Deposits:		
Food/Groceries:		
Other:		
Totals:		
OTHER:		
Guests		
Pets		

SIGNATURE:_____   _____

DATE:_____   _____

Objective # 9

Choose your roommates wisely: *Write out and agree upon house rules and responsibilities including costs - before moving in with anyone. Every roommate signs the agreement*

HOUSE RULES AND RESPONSIBILITIES: I (we) agree to abide by the following house rules:

CHORES AND RESPONSIBILITIES	NAME:	NAME:
Kitchen:		
Floors:		
Trash:		
Laundry:		
Other:		
EXPENSES:		
Rent:		
Utilities:		
Deposits:		
Food/Groceries:		
Other:		
Totals:		
OTHER:		
Guests		
Pets		

SIGNATURE:_____   _____

DATE:_____   _____

Objective # 10   Date(s):_____

Visit your neighborhood stores and ride bus lines you may use in the location you will live after you are on your own.

Pick up advertisements and bus or other potential transportation schedules. <u>Sign up for grocery store discount cards to save money on sale items</u>

Objective # 11   Date(s):_____

Furnish your kitchen and home inexpensively and practically.
Go to yard sales, thrift shops and look for new items on sale. Keep any receipts in your file box

Objective # 12   Date(s):_____

Create a computer file and/or an alphabetically organized file box for your regular monthly bills.

Purchase a file box with alphabetical inserts. Keep receipts for future reference; file them alphabetically

<u>Important Notes:</u>

    a. *Record the date, the check number and the amount paid on the portion you keep on every (paper) bill you pay

    b. *File your bills as soon as you write them out; keep for your records. If you pay online, check your deductions and balances at least twice a month. <u>If you have any questions or problems with your balance, call your bank and they will help you</u>*

    c. Staple or paper clip together your paper receipts. *At the end of each month, put them in a file marked RECEIPTS in your file box. Keep them paper clipped throughout the month in one place*

Objective # 13   Date(s):_____

Clean your house or apartment thoroughly at least three times per month. *If you have roommates, divide the work evenly and rotate chores*

Additional Notes and Information

Additional Notes and Information

"Let us make our future now,
And let us make our dreams
tomorrow's reality"

Malala Yausafzai

Additional Notes and Information

Additional Notes and Information

*"If we did all the things
we are capable of,
we would literally astound ourselves"*

Thomas A. Edison

INTERNSHIPS

Longmont Mural—courtesy of City of Longmont, CO and Gamma Acosta (artist)

Objective # 1:

Research Internship possibilities. *Check out more than one potential career before you commit to a career or education plan. Record information and good possibilities*

INTERNSHIP POSSIBILITY

Start Date: _____   **End Date:** _____

Business Name:

Business Address:

Telephone number/website:

Supervisor(s) name(s):

Referred by:

Your Internship Title:

Description of Internship:

Average number of hours to be worked per week:

Stipends or Wages:

Objective # 1:

Research Internship possibilities. *Check out more than one potential career before you commit to a career or education plan. Record information and good possibilities*

INTERNSHIP POSSIBILITY

Start Date: _____   End Date: _____

Business Name:

Business Address:

Telephone number/website:

Supervisor(s) name(s):

Referred by:

Your Internship Title:

Description of Internship:

Average number of hours to be worked per week:

Stipends or Wages:

Objective # 2:

Participate in Internship Placement <u>Field Trips</u>. *Try out several possibilities*

Record information.

INTERNSHIP FIELD TRIP

Date:

Business Name:

Business Address:

Telephone number/website:

Contact Person within Organization:

Field Trip Coordinator Information:

Potential Internship Title:

Description of Internship:

Average number of hours to be worked per week:

Stipends or Wages:

Objective # 2:

Participate in Internship Placement <u>Field Trips</u>. *Try out several possibilities*

Record information.

INTERNSHIP FIELD TRIP

Date:

Business Name:

Business Address:

Telephone number/website:

Contact Person within Organization:

Field Trip Coordinator Information:

Potential Internship Title:

Description of Internship:

Average number of hours to be worked per week:

Stipends or Wages:

Objective # 3:

Go on <u>Internship Placement Interviews.</u> * Completing more than one internship will help you to be much more informed when making career decisions. <u>Prepare for the Internship Placement Interview just as you would prepare for a regular job interview.</u> Research the organization and internship for which you are applying. Be prepared to tell them why they should pick you over other applicants; <u>be sincere, be yourself</u>*

Record information:

Internship Interviews

Date:

Business Name:

Business Address:

Telephone number/website:

Supervisor/Interviewer name(s):

Your Internship Title:

Description of Internship:

Average number of hours to be worked per week:

Stipends or Wages:

Objective # 3:

Go on <u>Internship Placement Interviews</u>. * <u>Take SMOOTH TRANSITIONS 4 TEENS with you when you fill out an application or interview for an internship.</u> All your information, which you will need, will be at your fingertips. Use SMOOTH TRANSITIONS 4 TEENS as your portfolio during the interview to <u>showcase the things you have been working on</u>*

Record information:

Internship Interviews

Date:

Business Name:

Business Address:

Telephone number/website:

Supervisor/Interviewer name(s):

Your Internship Title:

Description of Internship:

Average number of hours to be worked per week:

Stipends or Wages:

Objective # 4:

Practice your internship maintenance skills: appearance, punctuality, accuracy, working as a team member. *Consistently display excellent employment skills*

Objective # 5:

Successfully complete an internship. *Working as an intern can definitely help you get another paid position in the future. <u>Many employers look for or require potential employees to have internship experience and sometimes hire successful interns as paid employees</u>*

Record experiences:

INTERNSHIP

Start Date: _____   End Date: _____

Business Name:

Business Address:

Telephone number/website:

Supervisor name(s):

Your Internship Title:

Description of Internship:

Average number of hours worked per week:

Stipends or Wages:

Objective # 5:

Successfully complete an internship. *<u>Internships can be a big boost when applying for higher education opportunities</u>*

Record experiences:

INTERNSHIP

Start Date: _____   **End Date:** _____

Business Name:

Business Address:

Telephone number/website:

Supervisor name(s):

Your Internship Title:

Description of Internship:

Average number of hours worked per week:

Stipends or Wages:

Objective # 6:

Meet people with experience in your internship field of interest. *Ask around, <u>you can learn a lot by speaking with someone who has already interned for an organization</u>*

Record information:

NAME: DATE: _____

ADDRESS:

TELEPHONE NUMBER:

EMAIL/SOCIAL MEDIA:

RELATIONSHIP:

EXPERIENCES:

NAME: DATE: _____

ADDRESS:

TELEPHONE NUMBER:

EMAIL/SOCIAL MEDIA:

RELATIONSHIP:

EXPERIENCES:

Objective # 6:

Meet people with experience in your internship field of interest.

Record information:

NAME: DATE: _____

ADDRESS:

TELEPHONE NUMBER:

EMAIL/SOCIAL MEDIA:

RELATIONSHIP:

EXPERIENCES:

NAME: DATE: _____

ADDRESS:

TELEPHONE NUMBER:

EMAIL/SOCIAL MEDIA:

RELATIONSHIP:

EXPERIENCES:

Additional Notes and Information

"What lies behind you and what lies in front of you

pales in comparison to what lies inside of you"

Ralph Waldo Emerson

"True listening goes far beyond auditory perception.
It is the arising of alert attention,
A space of presence in which words are being received"

Eckhart Tolle

INTERPERSONAL SKILLS

Longmont Mural—courtesy of City of Longmont, CO and Gamma Acosta (artist)

Objective # 1:

Think about what your needs are and how to get them met.

* <u>Set aside some quiet time for yourself to look within</u>. Watch YouTube and other videos featuring speakers you admire about this topic*

My Need	How I will get my need met
1.	
2.	

Objective # 1:

Think about what your needs are and how to get them met.

Take some quiet time to think; take your time, go within, <u>be honest with yourself and decide how you can improve</u>

My Need	How I will get my need met

3.

4.

Objective # 2: Date(s):_____

Commit to respecting the needs of others. Talk to a trusted friend about this subject.

Think about how you want others to respect you and your needs and be that way toward them. <u>People will often look out for you and what you need because they observe you acting that way toward others</u>

Make notes:

"If your only tool is a hammer
you will see every problem
as a nail"

Abraham Maslow

Objective # 3:

Practice asserting yourself. Stand up for <u>your rights positively</u> and assume <u>your responsibilities.</u> Take responsibility for yourself first. *Speak in <u>I statements</u> as much as possible rather than blaming people, even if you believe you are right. How your message is sent is more important than how it is received*

Make notes:

Objective # 4:

Choose to resolve conflicts peacefully, give up the need to be right. Give space, cool down, speak your truth without attacking. *Develop the skill of being able to let go of an outcome. <u>Sometimes it is better not to engage, to allow and just observe what is</u>*

"To stand up for justice and peace, then, you must first find peace within yourself. You must then demonstrate peace to others, which means you can't make a stand for peace while you are warring with your neighbor, hating your coworker, or judging your boss."

Dr. Joe Dispenza

Notes:

Objective # 5:

Decide to relate and work well with your employers, co-workers, teachers, schoolmates, friends, etc.

If you have an issue with someone, talk to them about it in a respectful and direct manner. Maintain eye contact and no matter the response, keep your cool. <u>Deal with issues when they occur, if possible, rather than letting things go.</u> Small problems can unnecessarily grow into bigger problems by waiting. Many times, it is only a matter of miscommunication

Record your successes:

Additional Notes and Information

"Try to be the rainbow

In someone's cloud"

Maya Angelou

*"Do not forget small kindnesses
and
do not remember small faults"*

Chinese Proverb

"If we could read the secret history of our enemies,
We should find in each man's life
Sorrow and suffering enough
To disarm all hostility"

Henry Wadsworth Longfellow

"Tolerance comes of age.
I see no fault committed
that I myself
could not have committed
at some time or other."

Johann Wolfgang von Goethe

LEGAL ISSUES

Objective # 1:

Create your alphabetically organized and <u>lockable file box</u> to store <u>copies</u> of important documents so you will have a backup. Keep it in a safe place.

Keep the <u>original documents</u> listed below that you do not need to carry with you in a <u>locked security box,</u> stored in a secure place.

* <u>Protect your identity, keep your documents private and safe. Avoid giving personal financial information unless you initiate a transaction. Never use unsecured wifi to do any financial transaction. Never carry your social security card and only give the number when you are absolutely sure it is safe and required</u> *

DOCUMENT NAME	AGENCY CONTACT INFORMATION
Birth Certificate	
Social Security Card	
State Identity Card or Student ID	
Driver's License	
Work Permit (if required)	

Objective # 1:

Create your alphabetically organized and <u>lockable file box</u> to store <u>copies</u> of important documents so you will have a backup.

Keep it locked and in a safe place. Keep the <u>original documents</u> listed below that you do not need to carry with you <u>in a locked security box</u> stored in a secure place.

DOCUMENT NAME	AGENCY CONTACT INFORMATION
School Transcripts/ High School Diploma/ GED	
Other Degrees or Certificates	
Medical Records	
Registration for Selective Service, military service at age 18 (Males only)	

<u>Register to Vote at your local county courthouse.</u> *Bring your ID and proof of residence to register and obtain your Voter Registration Card. Know election dates and <u>your designated</u> local voting location. Study up on the candidates, <u>be an active participant in democracy and VOTE</u>*

Other Documents:

Additional Notes and Information

"The best preparation for
TOMORROW
Is doing your best
TODAY"

H. Jackson Brown, Jr.

Additional Notes and Information:

"Every morning cries to us:
Do what you ought
And trust what may be".

Johann Wolfgang Von Goethe

Additional Notes and Information:

LEISURE AND RECREATION

Objective # 1:

Do any kind of exercise you enjoy five times a week.

List activities:

Objective # 2:   Date(s):_____ _____

Enter recreation activities you participate in on <u>your</u> calendar.

Objective # 3:

Check online- research available local recreation possibilities that interest you.

Spend time in nature walking, exploring parks, hiking trails, biking etc. You may be interested in zumba or yoga classes, basketball, racquetball or other inside recreation, especially on rainy days or when the weather is extreme. <u>You will certainly meet active, friendly people, while boosting your mood and taking good care of your body</u>

Objective #4:

Join a team or volunteer to help a sports or recreation group. *<u>This is a great way to meet people, make friends and have fun</u>*

Record information:

Objective # 5:

Learn how to swim or become a better swimmer.

You could save your life or the life of someone else one day. Swimming is also a great way to relieve tension and decrease aches and pains

Notes:

Objective # 6:

Go camping and learn your survival skills.

Learn how to build a campfire, to cook over the fire, set up a tent, and chop wood. Check out videos on how to read a compass, a map, and take time to connect with nature and enjoy the outdoors

Record dates, locations and skills learned:

Objective # 7:

Find positive, new, creative recreation outlets for yourself.

Hike, bike, swim, kayak, jog, shoot hoops, walk dogs or play with kittens at an animal shelter, coach, mentor kids, golf, play ping pong or tennis, weightlift, play soccer, baseball...

Record your activities:

Objective # 8:

Take time to read, write, journal, draw, paint, rest, relax and just enjoy silence.

Use your time well. <u>Pace yourself, you have enough time</u>

Objective # 9:

Reserve a quiet time for yourself each day <u>without electronics</u>. Take a walk, slow down, meditate, visualize, pray, or take a nap when you need to. *Take at least 15 minutes a day to be in nature, in a park, near water, on a trail, or outside somewhere to be still, to center yourself, <u>to just be</u>*

Additional Notes and Information

*"Don't let the fear
of striking out
hold you back"*

Babe Ruth

MONEY MANAGEMENT

Objective # 1:

Write out your monthly budget. Subtract expenses from income. *When things change, write out a new budget; <u>subtract your expenses from your total income</u>*

Record below:

MONTHLY BUDGET

<u>EXPENSE</u>	<u>ENTRY</u>	AMOUNT <u>SPENT</u>
Savings		
Food		
Rent		
Electric		
Gas/ Water/Sewer		
Cable/Satellite		
Phone/ Cell Phone		
WiFi/ Internet access		
Health/Dental Insurance		
Medical/Dental Bills		
Credit Card payment		
Car Insurance		
Car Payment		
Car Maintenance		
Gasoline		
Clothing		
Entertainment		
Other		

ALL SOURCES OF MONTHLY INCOME   _____

MONTHLY EXPENSES   _____

TOTAL   _____

Objective # 1:

Write out your monthly budget. Subtract expenses from income. *When things change, write out a new budget; <u>subtract your expenses from your total income</u>*

Record below:

MONTHLY BUDGET

<u>EXPENSE</u>	<u>ENTRY</u>	AMOUNT <u>SPENT</u>
Savings		
Food		
Rent		
Electric		
Gas/ Water/Sewer		
Cable/Satellite		
Phone/ Cell Phone		
WiFi/ Internet access		
Health/Dental Insurance		
Medical/Dental Bills		
Credit Card payment		
Car Insurance		
Car Payment		
Car Maintenance		
Gasoline		
Clothing		
Entertainment		
Other		

ALL SOURCES OF MONTHLY INCOME _____

—

MONTHLY EXPENSES _____

TOTAL _____

Objective # 2:

Practice balancing an imaginary checkbook. Create monthly scenarios for yourself. *
Include paycheck and other deposits, expenses, including rent, electric, phone, gas, other
bills, etc. <u>Talk to someone with experience and ask for help</u>. Check out online banking;
balance your account monthly. Use online videos to train yourself*

Check Number	Date	Description of Transaction	Payment or Withdrawal		Fee (+/-)	Deposit/Credit or Interest		Balance	

Objective # 2:

Practice balancing an imaginary checkbook. Create monthly scenarios for yourself. * Include paycheck deposits and other deposits, expenses, including rent, electric, phone, gas, other bills, etc. <u>Talk to someone with experience and ask for help</u>. Check out online banking; balance your account monthly. Use online videos to train yourself*

Check Number	Date	Description of Transaction	Payment or Withdrawal		Fee (+/-)	Deposit/Credit or Interest		Balance	

Objective # 3   Date: _____

Open a savings account and/or an interest checking account for yourself.

*Save a minimum of 25% of your income each month if someone else is paying your bills.
Otherwise do your best to save 10% each month.

Write out a savings plan*

MY SAVINGS PLAN

My age now: _____

Number of months until I will be on my own;
Use the calendars at the back of the book   _____

Total number of months worked   _____

Dollars per month I will save =   _____

Additional money saved from extra hours worked;
i.e., additional summer work hours, overtime,
other sources   _____

            TOTAL   _____

Objective # 4   Date(s):_____

Commit to paying your bills on time.

*<u>Keep a record of bills you have paid</u>. If you are ever billed for something you have already paid for, you will have a written or electronic record of it to prove you have paid the bill.

Check your paycheck deductions for accuracy regularly. Keep your check stubs in your file box if you get a paper check stub*

Objective # 5:

Learn about establishing credit.

Do online research and talk to people you trust about the benefits, risks and wise use of credit

Record:

Objective # 6:

Establish credit by age 21. You will need credit to rent a hotel room, rent a car or buy anything which you pay for over time, such as furniture, a car, a house, etc.

*Avoid paying interest on balances. Pay off your bill every month to establish good credit and boost your credit rating. Charge only what you must and are able to pay off before the bill comes due.

Your credit score is a number which is calculated by banks or other lending agencies to determine if you are a good credit risk based on your credit history. You need to establish a credit history*

Notes:

*"The measure of
who we are is
what we do with
what we have"*

Vince Lombardi

Additional Notes and Information

"Self-Actualizing people must be what they can be."

Abraham Maslow

PERSONAL OBJECTIVES

Objective # 1:   **Date:**

* Think and Create*

Objective # 2:   **Date:**

Create and Be

Objective # 3:   **Date:**

Be and Express Yourself

Objective # 4:   **Date:**

Express Yourself and Experience Life with Joy

Objective # 5:   **Date:**

Experience Life; Get to Know Who You Are

Objective # 6:   **Date:**

You Are What You Think

"Nothing is impossible,
the word itself says
I'M POSSIBLE"

Audrey Hepburn

Additional Notes and Information

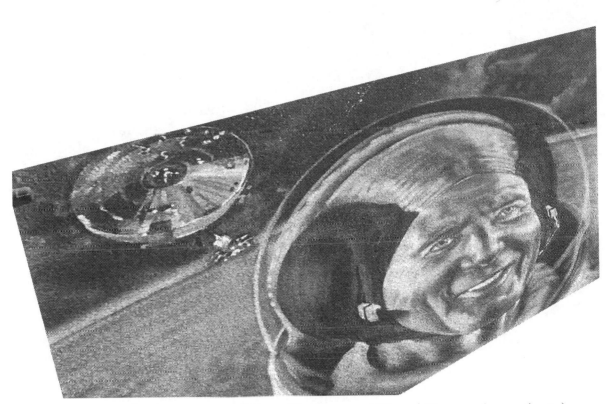

Longmont Mural—courtesy of City of Longmont, CO and Gamma Acosta (artist)

"If a person does not keep pace with his or her companions,
perhaps it is because he or she
hears a different drummer.
Let him or her step to the music which they hear,
however measured or far away"

Henry David Thoreau

"This is a time in history
When it is not enough
To simply know;
This is a time to know how"

Dr. Joe Dispenza

Additional Notes and Information

*"When you are inspired…
you discover yourself to be
a greater person by far
than you ever dreamed
yourself to be".*

Dr. Wayne W. Dyer

SUPPORT NETWORK

Objective # 1:

Check online and read your local Sunday newspaper weekly to keep informed. Be on the lookout for things you might like to participate in.

Whether you are looking for something to do such as checking out sporting events, festivals, free thing to do, parks to visit, concerts, tours, where to buy something, educational events, kids' events…, you can usually find something in the Sunday paper or online. <u>Get out and explore, try out a variety of things</u>

Notes:

Objective # 2:

Spend time twice a month or more with someone you admire.

Describe your experiences; write about the qualities you admire about this person.

When you show sincere interest in and demonstrate respect for someone who has accomplished good things in their life by asking questions and really listening, <u>you can learn so much.</u> You could create a lifelong friendship, and age difference does not matter. <u>Choose to engage with the purpose of learning</u>

Include names, dates, experiences:

Objective # 3:

Record phone numbers and addresses of your local human services offices, such as emergency food stamps (if needed), health care benefits, legal aid services, etc.

This could include your local county Department of Human Services, your health care insurance provider, Urgent Care clinics, free medical clinics and free legal advice. Check online

Objective # 4:

Join a support group specific to an area in which you may need support.

Check online, in your newspaper or at a church or school.

*There are lots of groups where you can feel supported in addition to traditional support groups like alcoholics anonymous, substance abuse groups or counseling.

These could be sports groups like kayaking, tennis, volleyball, etc., or civic groups such as the Rotary, Lions…, reading clubs, computer groups, church groups, travel clubs…*

Record information:

Objective # 5:

Do one thing each day to help others. <u>Actively choose to accomplish this every day.</u>
Watch your support network grow around you.

*The law of attraction says you create for yourself what you give to others.
<u>Try it, you will be amazed</u>*

Keep a record:

Objective # 6:

Seek out opportunities to actively support things you believe in. <u>Give what you need</u> <u>and</u>
<u>you will receive!</u>

*An excellent way to receive support and to build your support network is to give support.
<u>Offer your support to others</u> <u>and you will usually receive support in return as a byproduct of</u>
<u>your efforts.</u> Examples; help with tree planting projects, trail building, community gardens,
assisting elderly or others in need...*

"Projects that connect young people
Productively with other youth and adults
Are now seen to be the foundations
Upon which healthy communities can be built".

John P. Kretzmann and John McKnight

"Youth can always make a significant contribution
To the development of the communities
In which they live.
What is needed for this to happen
Are specific projects that will connect youth with the community."

John P. Kretzmann and John McKnight

TRANSPORTATION

Objective #1:

Go online to check out public transportation if you need it. Find out about monthly passes and schedules.

If you are enrolled in any post high school education, delaying buying a car while in school could help you stay focused on your course work without the expense of purchasing, insuring and maintaining a car. This also helps with decreasing student loan debt. <u>If you know someone with a car offer to help pay for gas to get where you want to go</u>

Notes, Date(s):

Objective # 2   Date: _____

Get your driver's license by age 18, while still in high school, if possible.

Many schools provide free or very low-cost classroom and behind the wheel drivers ed

Information, dates:

Objective # 3   Date: _____

Research car buying: check **blue-book** (average buying and selling prices for cars based on age, condition, etc.) values online.

*Compare- shop around before you buy anything; take your time; talk to people you trust who are experienced in car buying.
<u>Know the total cost of your car, including any interest costs. This amount is what the car really costs</u>*

Notes:

Objective # 4:   Date: _____

Research automobile insurance. Go online and call about several rate quotes before you buy a car; shop around.

<u>Talk to people you trust, ask them where they buy insurance and what their experiences have been</u>

Notes:

Objective # 5: Date: _____

Get to know a good mechanic. Check online reviews, ask around, talk to friends and family.

Have your mechanic check out a car before you buy it. <u>Resist the temptation to buy anything before you take the time to shop around to compare prices, models and costs of maintaining a car you are interested in buying</u>. You will be glad you did!

Record information:

Objective # 6 Date(s): _____

Read the owner's manual for the car you purchase. Keep it in your glove compartment.

Become familiar with your car.

* Make sure you keep your car serviced. Scheduled service times for oil changes, transmission, engine coolant etc. are listed in your owner's manual. <u>Spending the money to keep your car serviced will save on costly repairs caused by neglect.</u> Your car will last a lot longer and you will save money in the long run*

Additional Notes and Information

"All our dreams can come true
If we have the
courage to pursue them"

Walt Disney

Additional Notes and Information

Additional Notes and Information

"They can because they think they can."

Virgil

VOLUNTEERING

Objective # 1

Research volunteer possibilities. Check out career options through volunteering before you commit to a career or education plan. * Examples: volunteer to help out a veterinarian, at a food bank or a soup kitchen, help an elderly neighbor in need, assist in disaster relief efforts in some way, participate in neighborhood cleanup projects, mentor a peer or younger student ...*

Record:

Volunteer Possibilities

The more possibilities you check out, the more choices you will have

Volunteer Site Name:

Volunteer Site Address:

Volunteer Site Contact Information (website, phone number):

Supervisor Name(s):

Volunteer Coordinator:

Position Title:

Description of Responsibilities:

Number of hours per week/month:

Wages/Stipend:

Objective # 1

Research volunteer possibilities. *Check out career options through volunteering before you commit to an education plan. <u>The people you volunteer with may have had many other previous career experiences which you can learn about</u>. The more possibilities you check out, the more choices you will have*

Record:

Volunteer Possibilities

Volunteer Site Name:

Volunteer Site Address:

Volunteer Site Contact Information (website, phone number):

Supervisor Name(s):

Volunteer Coordinator:

Position Title:

Description of Responsibilities:

Number of hours per week/month:

Wages/Stipend:

Objective # 2   Date(s):_____

<u>Participate</u> in volunteer placement <u>field trips</u>. *Try out several possibilities and see what feels comfortable to you*

Record information:

Volunteer Placement Field Trips

Volunteer Site Name:

Volunteer Site Address:

Volunteer Site Telephone Number:

Volunteer Site Contact Information (website, phone number):

Supervisor Name(s):

Volunteer Coordinator:

Position Title:

Description of Responsibilities:

Number of hours per week/month:

Wages/Stipend:

Objective # 2   Date(s):_____

<u>Participate</u> in volunteer placement <u>field trips</u>. Try out several possibilities and see what feels comfortable to you. A field trip will allow you to quickly eliminate some choices or move forward with an option which feels good to you*

Record information:

Volunteer Placement Field Trips

Volunteer Site Name:

Volunteer Site Address:

Volunteer Site Telephone Number:

Volunteer Site Contact Information (website, phone number):

Supervisor Name(s):

Volunteer Coordinator:

Position Title:

Description of Responsibilities:

Number of hours per week/month:

Wages/Stipend:

Objective # 3:

Go on volunteer placement <u>interviews</u>.

*Take <u>SMOOTH TRANSITIONS 4 TEENS</u> with you. <u>Tell what you have accomplished and show them the plans you have been working on.</u> Be prepared to explain why you would like to volunteer.

Present yourself with a smile and humility*

Describe each experience. Record dates:

Go on volunteer placement <u>interviews.</u>

Describe the experience. Record dates:

Objective # 4   Date(s):_____

<u>Carry out</u> your volunteer work, possibly with a mentor, 3 or more hours per month.

Try a variety of volunteer opportunities. <u>You will meet great people and have opportunities to experiment with potential education and career options. Be sure to include your volunteer work in your resume</u>`

Volunteer Work

Describe experiences and record information:

Volunteer Site Name:

Volunteer Site Address:

Volunteer Site Telephone Number:

Volunteer Site Contact Information (website, email):

Supervisor Name(s):

Volunteer Coordinator:

Position Title:

Description of Responsibilities:

Number of hours per week/month:

Wages/Stipend:

Objective # 4   Date(s):_____

<u>Carry out</u> your volunteer work, possibly with a mentor, 3 or more hours per month. Try a variety of volunteer opportunities. <u>Volunteering looks great on a resume' and could connect you with paid job opportunities</u>*

Describe experiences and record information:

Volunteer Work

Volunteer Site Name:

Volunteer Site Address:

Volunteer Site Telephone Number:

Volunteer Site Contact Information (website, email):

Supervisor Name(s):

Volunteer Coordinator:

Position Title:

Description of Responsibilities:

Number of hours per week/month:

Wages/Stipend:

Objective # 5:

Practice volunteer maintenance skills: appearance, accuracy, punctuality, working as a team member. *<u>The qualities of character you display will speak volumes about the kind of person you are. People will take notice of the employment skills you regularly demonstrate</u> *

Notes:

Objective # 6:

Ask for letters of reference for future employment or academic needs before you leave a volunteer site.

* <u>Thank those you have volunteered with for the opportunity to work alongside them. If you think it is appropriate certain fellow volunteers might be a good source for letters of reference</u>*

Record information and date(s):

"I slept and dreamt that life was joy.
I awoke and saw that life was service.
I acted and behold,
Service was joy."

Tagore

*"A hero is someone who
has given his or her life
to something bigger than oneself"*

Joseph Campbell

Additional Notes and Information

Additional Notes and Information

MONTHLY PLANS

MONTHLY PLANS

 # 1   **Month:**   **Year:**

WEEK # 1:

WEEK # 2:

WEEK # 3:

WEEK # 4:

WEEK # 5:

MONTHLY PLANS

2   Month: Year:

WEEK # 1:

WEEK # 2:

WEEK # 3:

WEEK # 4:

WEEK # 5:

MONTHLY PLANS

 # 3   **Month:**   **Year:**

WEEK # 1:

WEEK # 2:

WEEK # 3:

WEEK # 4:

WEEK # 5:

MONTHLY PLANS

4   Month: Year:

WEEK # 1:

WEEK # 2:

WEEK # 3:

WEEK # 4:

WEEK # 5:

MONTHLY PLANS

5   Month: Year:

WEEK # 1:

WEEK # 2:

WEEK # 3:

WEEK # 4:

WEEK # 5:

MONTHLY PLANS

6

Month: **Year:**

<u>WEEK # 1:</u>

<u>WEEK # 2:</u>

<u>WEEK # 3:</u>

<u>WEEK # 4:</u>

<u>WEEK # 5:</u>

MONTHLY PLANS

#7   **Month:**   **Year:**

WEEK # 1:

WEEK # 2:

WEEK # 3:

WEEK # 4:

WEEK # 5:

MONTHLY PLANS

8   Month: Year:

WEEK # 1:

WEEK # 2:

WEEK # 3:

WEEK # 4:

WEEK # 5:

MONTHLY PLANS

9   Month: Year:

WEEK # 1:

WEEK # 2:

WEEK # 3:

WEEK # 4:

WEEK # 5:

MONTHLY PLANS

10   Month: Year:

WEEK # 1:

WEEK # 2:

WEEK # 3:

WEEK # 4:

WEEK # 5:

MONTHLY PLANS

11   Month: Year:

<u>WEEK # 1:</u>

<u>WEEK # 2:</u>

<u>WEEK # 3:</u>

<u>WEEK # 4:</u>

<u>WEEK # 5:</u>

MONTHLY PLANS

12   **Month:**   **Year:**

WEEK # 1:

WEEK # 2:

WEEK # 3:

WEEK # 4:

WEEK # 5:

MONTHLY PLANS

13   Month: Year:

WEEK # 1:

WEEK # 2:

WEEK # 3:

WEEK # 4:

WEEK # 5:

MONTHLY PLANS

14   Month: Year:

WEEK # 1:

WEEK # 2:

WEEK # 3:

WEEK # 4:

WEEK # 5:

MONTHLY PLANS

15   Month: Year:

WEEK # 1:

WEEK # 2:

WEEK # 3:

WEEK # 4:

WEEK # 5:

MONTHLY PLANS

16   Month: Year:

WEEK # 1:

WEEK # 2:

WEEK # 3:

WEEK # 4:

WEEK # 5:

MONTHLY PLANS

17   Month: Year:

WEEK # 1:

WEEK # 2:

WEEK # 3:

WEEK # 4:

WEEK # 5:

MONTHLY PLANS

18   Month: Year:

WEEK # 1:

WEEK # 2:

WEEK # 3:

WEEK # 4:

WEEK # 5:

MONTHLY PLANS

19   Month: Year:

<u>WEEK # 1:</u>

<u>WEEK # 2:</u>

<u>WEEK # 3:</u>

<u>WEEK # 4:</u>

<u>WEEK # 5:</u>

MONTHLY PLANS

20   **Month:**   **Year:**

WEEK # 1:

WEEK # 2:

WEEK # 3:

WEEK # 4:

WEEK # 5:

MONTHLY PLANS

21   Month: Year:

WEEK # 1:

WEEK # 2:

WEEK # 3:

WEEK # 4:

WEEK # 5:

MONTHLY PLANS

22   **Month:**   **Year:**

WEEK # 1:

WEEK # 2:

WEEK # 3:

WEEK # 4:

WEEK # 5:

MONTHLY PLANS

23   Month: Year:

WEEK # 1:

WEEK # 2:

WEEK # 3:

WEEK # 4:

WEEK # 5:

MONTHLY PLANS

24   **Month:**   **Year:**

WEEK # 1:

WEEK # 2:

WEEK # 3:

WEEK # 4:

WEEK # 5:

YEARLY CALENDARS

JANUARY 2018

S	M	T	W	TH	F	S
	1	2	3	4	5	6
7	8	9	10	11	12	13
14	15	16	17	18	19	20
21	22	23	24	25	26	27
28	29	30	31			

FEBRUARY 2018

S	M	T	W	TH	F	S
				1	2	3
4	5	6	7	8	9	10
11	12	13	14	15	16	17
18	19	20	21	22	23	24
25	26	27	28			

MARCH 2018

S	M	T	W	TH	F	S
				1	2	3
4	5	6	7	8	9	10
11	12	13	14	15	16	17
18	19	20	21	22	23	24
25	26	27	28	29	30	31

APRIL 2018

S	M	T	W	TH	F	S
1	2	3	4	5	6	7
8	9	10	11	12	13	14
15	16	17	18	19	20	21
22	23	24	25	26	27	28
29	30					

MAY 2018

S	M	T	W	TH	F	S
		1	2	3	4	5
6	7	8	9	10	11	12
13	14	15	16	17	18	19
20	21	22	23	24	25	26
27	28	29	30	31		

JUNE 2018

S	M	T	W	TH	F	S
					1	2
3	4	5	6	7	8	9
10	11	12	13	14	15	16
17	18	19	20	21	22	23
24	25	26	27	28	29	30

JULY 2018

S	M	T	W	TH	F	S
1	2	3	4	5	6	7
8	9	10	11	12	13	14
15	16	17	18	19	20	21
22	23	24	25	26	27	28
29	30	31				

AUGUST 2018

S	M	T	W	TH	F	S
			1	2	3	4
5	6	7	8	9	10	11
12	13	14	15	16	17	18
19	20	21	22	23	24	25
26	27	28	29	30	31	

SEPTEMBER 2018

S	M	T	W	TH	F	S
						1
2	3	4	5	6	7	8
9	10	11	12	13	14	15
16	17	18	19	20	21	22
23	24	25	26	27	28	29
30						

OCTOBER 2018

S	M	T	W	TH	F	S
	1	2	3	4	5	6
7	8	9	10	11	12	13
14	15	16	17	18	19	20
21	22	23	24	25	26	27
28	29	30	31			

NOVEMBER 2018

S	M	T	W	TH	F	S
				1	2	3
4	5	6	7	8	9	10
11	12	13	14	15	16	17
18	19	20	21	22	23	24
25	26	27	28	29	30	

DECEMBER 2018

S	M	T	W	TH	F	S
						1
2	3	4	5	6	7	8
9	10	11	12	13	14	15
16	17	18	19	20	21	22
23	24	25	26	27	28	29
30	31					

JANUARY 2019

S	M	T	W	TH	F	S
		1	2	3	4	5
6	7	8	9	10	11	12
13	14	15	16	17	18	19
20	21	22	23	24	25	26
27	28	29	30	31		

FEBRUARY 2019

S	M	T	W	TH	F	S
					1	2
3	4	5	6	7	8	9
10	11	12	13	14	15	16
17	18	19	20	21	22	23
24	25	26	27	28		

MARCH 2019

S	M	T	W	TH	F	S
					1	2
3	4	5	6	7	8	9
10	11	12	13	14	15	16
17	18	19	20	21	22	23
24	25	26	27	28	29	30
31						

APRIL 2019

S	M	T	W	TH	F	S
	1	2	3	4	5	6
7	8	9	10	11	12	13
14	15	16	17	18	19	20
21	22	23	24	25	26	27
28	29	30				

MAY 2019

S	M	T	W	TH	F	S
			1	2	3	4
5	6	7	8	9	10	11
12	13	14	15	16	17	18
19	20	21	22	23	24	25
26	27	28	29	30	31	

JUNE 2019

S	M	T	W	TH	F	S
						1
2	3	4	5	6	7	8
9	10	11	12	13	14	15
16	17	18	19	20	21	22
23	24	25	26	27	28	29
30						

JULY 2019

S	M	T	W	TH	F	S
	1	2	3	4	5	6
7	8	9	10	11	12	13
14	15	16	17	18	19	20
21	22	23	24	25	26	27
28	29	30	31			

AUGUST 2019

S	M	T	W	TH	F	S
				1	2	3
4	5	6	7	8	9	10
11	12	13	14	15	16	17
18	19	20	21	22	23	24
25	26	27	28	29	30	31

SEPTEMBER 2019

S	M	T	W	TH	F	S
1	2	3	4	5	6	7
8	9	10	11	12	13	14
15	16	17	18	19	20	21
22	23	24	25	26	27	28
29	30					

OCTOBER 2019

S	M	T	W	TH	F	S
		1	2	3	4	5
6	7	8	9	10	11	12
13	14	15	16	17	18	19
20	21	22	23	24	25	26
27	28	29	30	31		

NOVEMBER 2019

S	M	T	W	TH	F	S
					1	2
3	4	5	6	7	8	9
10	11	12	13	14	15	16
17	18	19	20	21	22	23
24	25	26	27	28	29	30

DECEMBER 2019

S	M	T	W	TH	F	S
1	2	3	4	5	6	7
8	9	10	11	12	13	14
15	16	17	18	19	20	21
22	23	24	25	26	27	28
29	30	31				

JANUARY 2020

S	M	T	W	TH	F	S
			1	2	3	4
5	6	7	8	9	10	11
12	13	14	15	16	17	18
19	20	21	22	23	24	25
26	27	28	29	30	31	

FEBRUARY 2020

S	M	T	W	TH	F	S
						1
2	3	4	5	6	7	8
9	10	11	12	13	14	15
16	17	18	19	20	21	22
23	24	25	26	27	28	29

MARCH 2020

S	M	T	W	TH	F	S
1	2	3	4	5	6	7
8	9	10	11	12	13	14
15	16	17	18	19	20	21
22	23	24	25	26	27	28
29	30	31				

APRIL 2020

S	M	T	W	TH	F	S
			1	2	3	4
5	6	7	8	9	10	11
12	13	14	15	16	17	18
19	20	21	22	23	24	25
26	27	28	29	30		

MAY 2020

S	M	T	W	TH	F	S
					1	2
3	4	5	6	7	8	9
10	11	12	13	14	15	16
17	18	19	20	21	22	23
24	25	26	27	28	29	30
31						

JUNE 2020

S	M	T	W	TH	F	S
	1	2	3	4	5	6
7	8	9	10	11	12	13
14	15	16	17	18	19	20
21	22	23	24	25	26	27
28	29	30				

JULY 2020

S	M	T	W	TH	F	S
			1	2	3	4
5	6	7	8	9	10	11
12	13	14	15	16	17	18
19	20	21	22	23	24	25
26	27	28	29	30	31	

AUGUST 2020

S	M	T	W	TH	F	S
						1
2	3	4	5	6	7	8
9	10	11	12	13	14	15
16	17	18	19	20	21	22
23	24	25	26	27	28	29
30	31					

SEPTEMBER 2020

S	M	T	W	TH	F	S
		1	2	3	4	5
6	7	8	9	10	11	12
13	14	15	16	17	18	19
20	21	22	23	24	25	26
27	28	29	30			

OCTOBER 2020

S	M	T	W	TH	F	S
				1	2	3
4	5	6	7	8	9	10
11	12	13	14	15	16	17
18	19	20	21	22	23	24
25	26	27	28	29	30	31

NOVEMBER 2020

S	M	T	W	TH	F	S
1	2	3	4	5	6	7
8	9	10	11	12	13	14
15	16	17	18	19	20	21
22	23	24	25	26	27	28
29	30					

DECEMBER 2020

S	M	T	W	TH	F	S
		1	2	3	4	5
6	7	8	9	10	11	12
13	14	15	16	17	18	19
20	21	22	23	24	25	26
27	28	29	30	31		

JANUARY 2021

S	M	T	W	TH	F	S
					1	2
3	4	5	6	7	8	9
10	11	12	13	14	15	16
17	18	19	20	21	22	23
24	25	26	27	28	29	30
31						

FEBRUARY 2021

S	M	T	W	TH	F	S
	1	2	3	4	5	6
7	8	9	10	11	12	13
14	15	16	17	18	19	20
21	22	23	24	25	26	27
28						

MARCH 2021

S	M	T	W	TH	F	S
	1	2	3	4	5	6
7	8	9	10	11	12	13
14	15	16	17	18	19	20
21	22	23	24	25	26	27
28	29	30	31			

APRIL 2021

S	M	T	W	TH	F	S
				1	2	3
4	5	6	7	8	9	10
11	12	13	14	15	16	17
18	19	20	21	22	23	24
25	26	27	28	29	30	

MAY 2021

S	M	T	W	TH	F	S
						1
2	3	4	5	6	7	8
9	10	11	12	13	14	15
16	17	18	19	20	21	22
23	24	25	26	27	28	29
30	31					

JUNE 2021

S	M	T	W	TH	F	S
		1	2	3	4	5
6	7	8	9	10	11	12
13	14	15	16	17	18	19
20	21	22	23	24	25	26
27	28	29	30			

JULY 2021

S	M	T	W	TH	F	S
				1	2	3
4	5	6	7	8	9	10
11	12	13	14	15	16	17
18	19	20	21	22	23	24
25	26	27	28	29	30	31

AUGUST 2021

S	M	T	W	TH	F	S
1	2	3	4	5	6	7
8	9	10	11	12	13	14
15	16	17	18	19	20	21
22	23	24	25	26	27	28
29	30	31				

SEPTEMBER 2021

S	M	T	W	TH	F	S
			1	2	3	4
5	6	7	8	9	10	11
12	13	14	15	16	17	18
19	20	21	22	23	24	25
26	27	28	29	30		

OCTOBER 2021

S	M	T	W	TH	F	S
					1	2
3	4	5	6	7	8	9
10	11	12	13	14	15	16
17	18	19	20	21	22	23
24	25	26	27	28	29	30
31						

NOVEMBER 2021

S	M	T	W	TH	F	S
	1	2	3	4	5	6
7	8	9	10	11	12	13
14	15	16	17	18	19	20
21	22	23	24	25	26	27
28	29	30				

DECEMBER 2021

S	M	T	W	TH	F	S
			1	2	3	4
5	6	7	8	9	10	11
12	13	14	15	16	17	18
19	20	21	22	23	24	25
26	27	28	29	30	31	

JANUARY 2022

S	M	T	W	TH	F	S
						1
2	3	4	5	6	7	8
9	10	11	12	13	14	15
16	17	18	19	20	21	22
23	24	25	26	27	28	29
30	31					

FEBRUARY 2022

S	M	T	W	TH	F	S
		1	2	3	4	5
6	7	8	9	10	11	12
13	14	15	16	17	18	19
20	21	22	23	24	25	26
27	28					

MARCH 2022

S	M	T	W	TH	F	S
		1	2	3	4	5
6	7	8	9	10	11	12
13	14	15	16	17	18	19
20	21	22	23	24	25	26
27	28	29	30	31		

APRIL 2022

S	M	T	W	TH	F	S
					1	2
3	4	5	6	7	8	9
10	11	12	13	14	15	16
17	18	19	20	21	22	23
24	25	26	27	28	29	30

MAY 2022

S	M	T	W	TH	F	S
1	2	3	4	5	6	7
8	9	10	11	12	13	14
15	16	17	18	19	20	21
22	23	24	25	26	27	28
29	30	31				

JUNE 2022

S	M	T	W	TH	F	S
			1	2	3	4
5	6	7	8	9	10	11
12	13	14	15	16	17	18
19	20	21	22	23	24	25
26	27	28	29	30		

JULY 2022

S	M	T	W	TH	F	S
					1	2
3	4	5	6	7	8	9
10	11	12	13	14	15	16
17	18	19	20	21	22	23
24	25	26	27	28	29	30
31						

AUGUST 2022

S	M	T	W	TH	F	S
	1	2	3	4	5	6
7	8	9	10	11	12	13
14	15	16	17	18	19	20
21	22	23	24	25	26	27
28	29	30	31			

SEPTEMBER 2022

S	M	T	W	TH	F	S
				1	2	3
4	5	6	7	8	9	10
11	12	13	14	15	16	17
18	19	20	21	22	23	24
25	26	27	28	29	30	

OCTOBER 2022

S	M	T	W	TH	F	S
						1
2	3	4	5	6	7	8
9	10	11	12	13	14	15
16	17	18	19	20	21	22
23	24	25	26	27	28	29
30	31					

NOVEMBER 2022

S	M	T	W	TH	F	S
		1	2	3	4	5
6	7	8	9	10	11	12
13	14	15	16	17	18	19
20	21	22	23	24	25	26
27	28	29	30			

DECEMBER 2022

S	M	T	W	TH	F	S
				1	2	3
4	5	6	7	8	9	10
11	12	13	14	15	16	17
18	19	20	21	22	23	24
25	26	27	28	29	30	31

JANUARY 2023

S	M	T	W	TH	F	S
1	2	3	4	5	6	7
8	9	10	11	12	13	14
15	16	17	18	19	20	21
22	23	24	25	26	27	28
29	30	31				

FEBRUARY 2023

S	M	T	W	TH	F	S
			1	2	3	4
5	6	7	8	9	10	11
12	13	14	15	16	17	18
19	20	21	22	23	24	25
26	27	28				

MARCH 2023

S	M	T	W	TH	F	S
			1	2	3	4
5	6	7	8	9	10	11
12	13	14	15	16	17	18
19	20	21	22	23	24	25
26	27	28	29	30	31	

APRIL 2023

S	M	T	W	TH	F	S
						1
2	3	4	5	6	7	8
9	10	11	12	13	14	15
16	17	18	19	20	21	22
23	24	25	26	27	28	29
30						

MAY 2023

S	M	T	W	TH	F	S
	1	2	3	4	5	6
7	8	9	10	11	12	13
14	15	16	17	18	19	20
21	22	23	24	25	26	27
28	29	30	31			

JUNE 2023

S	M	T	W	TH	F	S
				1	2	3
4	5	6	7	8	9	10
11	12	13	14	15	16	17
18	19	20	21	22	23	24
25	26	27	28	29	30	

JULY 2023

S	M	T	W	TH	F	S
						1
2	3	4	5	6	7	8
9	10	11	12	13	14	15
16	17	18	19	20	21	22
23	245	25	26	27	28	29
30	31					

AUGUST 2023

S	M	T	W	TH	F	S
		1	2	3	4	5
6	7	8	9	10	11	12
13	14	15	16	17	18	19
20	21	22	23	24	25	26
27	28	29	30	31		

SEPTEMBER 2023

S	M	T	W	TH	F	S
					1	2
3	4	5	6	7	8	9
10	11	12	13	14	15	16
17	18	19	20	21	22	23
24	25	26	27	28	29	30

OCTOBER 2023

S	M	T	W	TH	F	S
1	2	3	4	5	6	7
8	9	10	11	12	13	14
15	16	17	18	19	20	21
22	23	24	25	26	27	28
29	30	31				

NOVEMBER 2023

S	M	T	W	TH	F	S
			1	2	3	4
5	6	7	8	9	10	11
12	13	14	15	16	17	18
19	20	21	22	23	24	25
26	27	28	29	30		

DECEMBER 2023

S	M	T	W	TH	F	S
					1	2
3	4	5	6	7	8	9
10	11	12	13	14	15	16
17	18	19	20	21	22	23
24	25	26	27	28	29	30
31						

JANUARY 2024

S	M	T	W	TH	F	S
	1	2	3	4	5	6
7	8	9	10	11	12	13
14	15	16	17	18	19	20
21	22	23	24	25	26	27
28	29	30	31			

FEBRUARY 2024

S	M	T	W	TH	F	S
				1	2	3
4	5	6	7	8	9	10
11	12	13	14	15	16	17
18	19	20	21	22	23	24
25	26	27	28	29		

MARCH 2024

S	M	T	W	TH	F	S
					1	2
3	4	5	6	7	8	9
10	11	12	13	14	15	16
17	18	19	20	21	22	23
24	25	26	27	28	29	30
31						

APRIL 2024

S	M	T	W	TH	F	S
	1	2	3	4	5	6
7	8	9	10	11	12	13
14	15	16	17	18	19	20
21	22	23	24	25	26	27
28	29	30				

MAY 2024

S	M	T	W	TH	F	S
			1	2	3	4
5	6	7	8	9	10	11
12	13	14	15	16	17	18
19	20	21	22	23	24	25
26	27	28	29	30	31	

JUNE 2024

S	M	T	W	TH	F	S
						1
2	3	4	5	6	7	8
9	10	11	12	13	14	15
16	17	18	19	20	21	22
23	24	25	26	27	28	29
30						

JULY 2024

S	M	T	W	TH	F	S
	1	2	3	4	5	6
7	8	9	10	11	12	13
14	15	16	17	18	19	20
21	22	23	24	25	26	27
28	29	30	31			

AUGUST 2024

S	M	T	W	TH	F	S
				1	2	3
4	5	6	7	8	9	10
11	12	13	14	15	16	17
18	19	20	21	22	23	24
25	26	27	28	29	30	31

SEPTEMBER 2024

S	M	T	W	TH	F	S
1	2	3	4	5	6	7
8	9	10	11	12	13	14
15	16	17	18	19	20	21
22	23	24	25	26	27	28
29	30					

OCTOBER 2024

S	M	T	W	TH	F	S
		1	2	3	4	5
6	7	8	9	10	11	12
13	14	15	16	17	18	19
20	21	22	23	24	25	26
27	28	29	30	31		

NOVEMBER 2024

S	M	T	W	TH	F	S
					1	2
3	4	5	6	7	8	9
10	11	12	13	14	15	16
17	18	19	20	21	22	23
24	25	26	27	28	29	30

DECEMBER 2024

S	M	T	W	TH	F	S
1	2	3	4	5	6	7
8	9	10	11	12	13	14
15	16	17	18	19	20	21
22	23	24	25	26	27	28
29	30	31				

JANUARY 2025

S	M	T	W	TH	F	S
			1	2	3	4
5	6	7	8	9	10	11
12	13	14	15	16	17	18
19	20	21	22	23	24	25
26	27	28	29	30	31	

FEBRUARY 2025

S	M	T	W	TH	F	S
						1
2	3	4	5	6	7	8
9	10	11	12	13	14	15
16	17	18	19	20	21	22
23	24	25	26	27	28	

MARCH 2025

S	M	T	W	TH	F	S
						1
2	3	4	5	6	7	8
9	10	11	12	13	14	15
16	17	18	19	20	21	22
23	24	25	26	27	28	29
30	31					

APRIL 2025

S	M	T	W	TH	F	S
		1	2	3	4	5
6	7	8	9	10	11	12
13	14	15	16	17	18	19
20	21	22	23	24	25	26
27	28	29	30			

MAY 2025

S	M	T	W	TH	F	S
				1	2	3
4	5	6	7	8	9	10
11	12	13	14	15	16	17
18	19	20	21	22	23	24
25	26	27	28	29	30	31

JUNE 2025

S	M	T	W	TH	F	S
1	2	3	4	5	6	7
8	9	10	11	12	13	14
15	16	17	18	19	20	21
22	23	24	25	26	27	28
29	30					

JULY 2025

S	M	T	W	TH	F	S
		1	2	3	4	5
6	7	8	9	10	11	12
13	14	15	16	17	18	19
20	21	22	23	24	25	26
27	28	29	30	31		

AUGUST 2025

S	M	T	W	TH	F	S
					1	2
3	4	5	6	7	8	9
10	11	12	13	14	15	16
17	18	19	20	21	22	23
24	25	26	27	28	29	30

SEPTEMBER 2025

S	M	T	W	TH	F	S
	1	2	3	4	5	6
7	8	9	10	11	12	13
14	15	16	17	18	19	20
21	22	23	24	25	26	27
28	29	30				

OCTOBER 2025

S	M	T	W	TH	F	S
			1	2	3	4
5	6	7	8	9	10	11
12	13	14	15	16	17	18
19	20	21	22	23	24	25
26	27	28	29	30	31	

NOVEMBER 2025

S	M	T	W	TH	F	S
						1
2	3	4	5	6	7	8
9	10	11	12	13	14	15
16	17	18	19	20	21	22
23	24	25	26	27	28	29
30						

DECEMBER 2025

S	M	T	W	TH	F	S
	1	2	3	4	5	6
7	8	9	10	11	12	13
14	15	16	17	18	19	20
21	22	23	24	25	26	27
28	29	30	31			

DRY MEASUREMENTS

3 teaspoons (tsp.) = 1 tablespoon (T.)
8 ounces (oz.) = 1 cup (c.)
16 ounces (oz.) = 1 pound (lb.)
2 cups (c.) = 1 pint(pt.)

LIQUID MEASURE

8 ounces (oz.) = 1 cup
2 cups (c.) = 1 pint (pt.) = 16 ounces (oz.)
2 pints (pts.) = 1 quart (qt.) = 32 ounces (oz.)
2 quarts (qts.) = ½ gallon (gal.) = 64 ounces (oz.)
4 quarts (qts.) = 1 gallon (gal.) = 128 ounces (oz.)
60 drops (gtts) = 1 teaspoon (tsp)

LINEAR MEASURE

12 inches (in.) = 1 foot (ft.)
3 feet (ft.) = 1 yard (yd.)
5,280 feet (ft.) = 1 mile
1,760 yards = 1 mile

METRIC CONVERSIONS

1 inch = 2.54 centimeters (cm.)   1 foot = .30 meters (mt.)
1 yard = .91 meters (mt.)

1 quart (dry) = 1.1 liters (L)   1 quart (liquid) = .94 liters (L)

2.2 pounds = 1 kilogram (kg)   1 gallon (liquid) = 3.78 liters (L)

.621 miles = 1 kilometer (Km)   1 acre = .404 hectares

Printed in the United States
By Bookmasters